JESUS CHRIST MADE SEATTLE UNDER PROTEST

poems by

Elaine S. Nussbaum

Finishing Line Press
Georgetown, Kentucky

JESUS CHRIST MADE SEATTLE UNDER PROTEST

Copyright © 2019 by Elaine S. Nussbaum
ISBN 978-1-64662-024-1 First Edition
All rights reserved under International and Pan-American Copyright Conventions. No part of this book may be reproduced in any manner whatsoever without written permission from the publisher, except in the case of brief quotations embodied in critical articles and reviews.

ACKNOWLEDGMENTS

Louisiana Literature: "Gefilte Fish"
Spilt Infinitive: "Jesus Christ Created Seattle Under Protest" and "Scotch"
Thimbleberry: "The Chiefs" and "Big Frog Clan"
Silk Road: "Salmon Spawning Sunday"

Many thanks to my teachers at Pacific University, especially Sandra Alcosser, Marvin Bell and Joe Millar. Also, my sincerest gratitude to my writing partners: Gwen McNeir, Kristina Hakanson, Karen Holman and Helen Gerhardt.

Publisher: Leah Maines
Editor: Christen Kincaid
Cover Art: Elaine S. Nussbaum
Author Photo: Zan Denise Hare
Cover Design: Elizabeth Maines McCleavy

Printed in the USA on acid-free paper.
Order online: www.finishinglinepress.com
also available on amazon.com

Author inquiries and mail orders:
Finishing Line Press
P. O. Box 1626
Georgetown, Kentucky 40324
U. S. A.

Table of Contents

Jesus Christ Made Seattle Under Protest

Jesus Christ Made Seattle Under Protest 1
Gefilte Fish 3
Scotch 4
Fly-fishing Circa 1918 5
Nisqually 6
The Third of July 12
Memorial Day, 2010 13
We Kicked Them Out of Paradise 14
Big Frog Clan 16
The Chiefs 18
How I Learned to Love the Mourning Dove Again 19
Jesús and the Colored Pencils 22
Inferno 24
A Slender Thread 25

Home

Home 29
This 30
As Each 31
Ant Sex 32
Is the Buddha Speaking? 33
Plum 34
The Struggle 35
Carnivore 36
Rooster (A Pantoum) 37
Salmon Spawning Sunday 38
Withered 39

Poems in the Key of Sea

Highway 30 43
Hood Canal 44
Willapa Bay, Beginning of June 45
Willapa Bay, End of August 46
Merroir/Eating Raw Oysters is Like Eating the Ocean 47
When I Came to the Desert I Didn't Think I Would
    Write a Poem About the Desert Sea 48
Monogamous 49
All the Sadness 50

Poem Written After Reading Stevens and Niedecker and
    Trying to Quit Coffee 51
Don't Turn Your Back on the Ocean 53
No Word of Want 54
Rubber Trees 56
Venus Disappearing 57

Twisted Little Love Songs

Flame 61
Gem #3 Beautiful Soul 62
Gem#4 Etta on the City of New Orleans 63
Gem#5 Greg 64
Gem#6 Sterling @ Antione's in the French Quarter 65
Gem#7 The Man in the Red Pork-Pie Hat 66
Gem#8 Uncle Louis 67
Gem#9 Tara in Camilla's Produce 68
A Love Like That 69
Ebu 70
US Citizen 71
Annabel 72
The Girl With Big Eyes 73
Jim on Father's Day 74
Tahoma 75
Black Ice 76

Bio

For David

JESUS CHRIST MADE
SEATTLE UNDER PROTEST

JESUS CHRIST MADE SEATTLE UNDER PROTEST

Jesus Christ Made Seattle Under Protest.
        That's how my mother taught me to remember
            the names of the streets.

Seattle—where my mother was born and my father.
        Where their parents immigrated.
            From Chicago, El Paso, San Francisco,

Boston. My great-grandparents: from Ireland, Germany,
        The Ukraine, Czechoslovakia. If you Google
            my grandfather's name you find a black

and white photo, a man in a long tweed
        coat holds a fedora at the grand opening
            of the Auburn Value Store—1960.

When my mother moved back to Seattle
        she lived in a one-bedroom walk-up
            with her African-American boyfriend.

My grandfather never spoke to her again.

I remember the smell of cat shit from the cat box
        and human shit from the bucket
            we emptied down the hall.

The one-eyed Norwegian landlord
        couldn't understand the photo of Huey Newton
            that hung above the bed, that iconic poster.

Newton sits in a high-backed rattan chair.
        He holds a rifle in one hand, a spear in the other.
            The chair rests on a zebra skin rug.

If you Google my mother's name you find
        a picture—Circa 1933. She is five, her brother three.
            The stand on a residential street wearing new school

clothes. The shadows are long, the sun catches
        the sides of their turned faces. My mother shades
                her eyes, and looks at something in the distance.

GEFILTE FISH

When Tantie's best friends died, so did the recipe for Gefilte fish.
Seven kinds of poached and ground fish—carp and pike and salmon
carefully chosen from those vendors at the Pike Place Market.
She knew 1/3 of the recipe and her best friends knew the other 2/3.

The tiny white kitchen, the hand crank. Each woman wears
a cotton apron embroidered with her initials, a net over blue hair.
Parsley and salt symbolize the tears of the Jews wandering
in the desert. The haroses, the mortar the Matzo, the unleavened
bread. The camellias outside the window explode scarletly.

After my mother left, my grandfather treated us to Thanksgiving
dinner at the Sheraton, or the Hilton so neither Gran Mollie
or Gran Minnie or Tantie had to cook. It was warm in the backseat
of the Buick, my pea-coat pulled tight to hide the run in my nylons.
I would see *them* sleeping on benches in lumpy gray clothing
or covered with tattered green blankets.

On weekends, I would hitchhike with my girlfriends to First and Pike
and *those men* would lumber towards us with their hands outstretched
and open their mouths with teeth missing, but just a very few white teeth
and it was so dark I would feel like I was falling into that dark hole.

SCOTCH

For my father, James Alfred Nussbaum

As the flesh falls away, his eyes appear sunken.
I notice: his prominent nose, how he breathes
through his open mouth despite pure oxygen
pumped into his lungs.

My sister leans on the fire-place mantle
wearing Dad's leather jacket, takes a sip
of scotch, tells the story: Grandma and Grandpa
on a train trip across the Midwest found
themselves next to Frank Lloyd Wright.

Nussbaum and Wright got into a heated discussion
and Wright asks him, *What the hell are you anyway?*
I'm a god-damned Irish-Jew. What are you going
to make of that, Wright.

*

His gums are purple, like he has been drinking wine.
He stays in the same upright position, though the cushions
that held his body, have been removed. Shortly before he died,
he asked my sister for a peanut butter sandwich.
Then he said, *Hell no, what I really want*
is a stiff drink of Scotch!

FLY-FISHING CIRCA 1918

For Minnie B. Stastny

Somewhere in Washington State, she
balances size four black lace-up leather
shoes on a single river rock.

The black leggings and wool knickers
are too warm for this spring afternoon.
Her dark hair which normally hangs
past her waist is tied up in a loose bun.

Fir and cedar line the banks where
osprey wait to catch the same steelhead
she hopes to catch. Snow melt

has swelled this river, singing
its own song on the way to the sea.

The earth smells like warm bark.
My grandmother grips the rod firmly,
but her shoulders are beginning
to hunch. She spots a flash in the river.

NISQUALLY

*For the 700 or more Water Protectors arrested
at Standing Rock, and the thousands still standing.*

1. FISH-IN @ FRANK'S LANDING—1966

I hear the drums. They have not stopped.
I heard them first when I was twelve.
A Volkswagen lurches up the driveway.

I heard them first when I was twelve.
I had not seen my mother in a year.
A peace symbol dangles from my neck.

I have not seen my mother in a year.
The peace symbol is red and blue. Painted
with house paint from my father's garage.

The peace symbol is red and blue.
Someone I don't know is driving.
As we get to the Rez sirens blare.

Someone I don't know is driving.
At the Rez, cars and trucks and boats
on trailers line the hard-packed road.

At the Rez cars and trucks and boats.
I open the door. Tear-gas streams in.
National Guard and State Police.

I open the door. Tear-gas streams in.
I hear gunshots. I cannot breathe.
I hear drumming and chanting.

I hear gunshots. I cannot breathe.
They will be fishing all night.
They are prepared to be arrested.

They will be fishing all night.
This war has been smoldering since 1864.
In 1966, they will be fishing all night.

The war has been smoldering since 1764.
I cannot breathe. Women with dark hair
and soft voices offer me fry bread.

I cannot breathe I see women with dark hair.
My mother finds me a soft place
by the Nisqually to unroll my sleeping bag.

My mother finds me a soft place to unroll my bag.
I fall asleep with soft rain washing my face.
I hear voices. I hear chanting.

I hear the swoosh of wind.
I hear the drums. Now I can breathe.

*

Their land stretched from mountain to ocean.
For 5,000 years they have fished.
The US squeezed them onto two square miles.

For 5,000 years they have fished.
Squally-absch means *The people of the grass country.*
Nisqually doesn't mean anything.

Squally-absch means *The people of the grass country.*
They picked berries in the mountains,
they caught salmon in the streams.

They picked berries in the mountains.
Tear gas obscures my vision.

My tears burn my throat.

The tear gas obscures my vision.
Article III gave them the right to fish
at all the accustomed grounds and stations.

Article III gave them the right to fish.
In 1945, Billy Frank was 14
when he was first arrested for fishing.

In 1945, Billy Frank was 14. In 1966,
he is joined by people from all over the country.
White, black and brown. Indian and non-Indian.

He is joined by people from all over the country.
They are all prepared to be arrested.
This is a war that has been raging since 1664.

They are all prepared to be arrested.
On the Nisqually, Puyallup, and Columbia
the Indians and their allies fished and got arrested.

On the Nisqually, Puyallup and Columbia.
George Bolt ruled in favor of the Nisqually.
He was a slight man and wore a bow tie.

George Bolt ruled in favor of the Nisqually:
a 50-50 division of fish between the Indians
and the white men who fished for sport and profit.

A 50-50 division of salmon and steel-head.
Bolt's decision has held up for 43 years.
In 2017, I suck on sweet smoked salmon.

Bolt's decision has held up for 43 years.
I suck on sweet smoked salmon
from a successful Native run fish market.

I hear the drums. They have not stopped.
I heard them first when I was twelve.

2. STANDING ROCK NORTH DAKOTA—2017

I have no native blood in me.
My heart pumps red the same as you.
Once again I hear the drums.

My heart pumps red the same as you.
I smell sage as I watch the news.
Water Protectors pray at Oceti Sakowin.

I smell sage as I watch the news.
100 Water Protectors remain and pray.
Humvees, M-Rats, and Bear Cats.

100 Water Protectors remain and pray.
Armored vehicles surround the camp.
Flags flap in the wind.

Armored vehicles surround the camp,
line the road. In the North Dakota winter
bare trees are stripped of their foliage,

line the road. In the North Dakota winter
Water Protectors face the east, the north,
the west, the south as spring rains begin.

Water Protectors face the east, the north.
Grandmothers are arrested while praying.
The rains begin, the floods are coming.

Grandmothers are arrested while praying.
Water protectors face the west, the south.
Police in riot gear storm the camp.

Water protectors face the west, the south.
Police search with automatic weapons drawn
as people smudge and pray.

Police search with automatic weapons drawn.
A man prays with eyes closed, sweeps smoke
from his smudge stick into the frigid air.

A man prays with eyes closed. Sweeps smoke.
His only protection is an upturned bed frame
and his prayers. He is surrounded.

His only protection an upturned bed frame.
They search structure to structure
like troops in Afghanistan or Iraq.

They search structure to structure: army
style mash tents, tipis, tarpees. Flames
shoot up in the night sky as structures burn.

Mash tents, tipis, tarpees. Flames shoot skyward
as the Water Protectors burn the structures
they have called home for months.

The Water Protectors burn the structures
they have lived in while fighting the Black Snake
prophesized by Lakota and Hopi legend.

They have been fighting the Black Snake
with prayer and song and community.
The Black Snake will slither across the Nation.

With prayer and song and community
they will slay the Black Snake which is
poisoning the water before destroying the earth.

They will slay the Black Snake called DAPL.

The Water Protectors have scattered to the four winds.
The seeds will take root and grow.

The Water Protectors have scattered to the four winds.
The last man at Standing Rock climbs a ladder,
asks *Did you know this is treaty land?*

The last man standing at Standing Rock climbs
a ladder to the top of a red roof. The treaty of 1851
promised this land to the Oceti Sakowin.

At the top of a building with a red roof
the last man at Standing Rock yells
Standing Rock will awaken the world!

THE THIRD OF JULY

The air conditioning in Walmart is controlled from Arkansas,
which normally would be fine, but here in Oregon it is ninety-nine,
ninety-one in the shade. The historic Civic Stadium in Eugene
has burned, and a housing development in Wenatchee. The man
on TV says *we got out so fast because we were scared.*
A glittering village at night, a pile of smoking rubble
the next morning. Eighteen major forest fires burn
in Oregon and Washington alone.

In the sweltering parking lot an older man wears
a straw cowboy hat, cut-offs and white knee socks.
He frowns. A robust blonde woman pulls
a dour faced little boy through the crosswalk.

On June 17, 2015, Dylann Roof massacred nine people
during Bible study at Charleston's Emanuel African Methodist
Episcopal Church. Roof's website and manifesto show him posing
with a Confederate flag, and since then at least five other
black churches have burned in the South, or maybe just
in South Carolina. Only one has been attributed to lightning.

A young black woman in South Carolina climbs a flagpole,
and removes the Confederate flag. *Enough is enough!* she says.
And in Oregon, lawmakers discuss removal of Mississippi's
Confederate-marked state flag from the state capitol building.
All across this burning nation, the Stars and Stripes wave
in the hot gray sky as we wait for that celebration
of the Star-spangled fireworks over urban cities and rural
towns, and hope that the whole damn thing doesn't go up in flames.

MEMORIAL DAY, 2010

1000 dead in Afghanistan. Beat poet Peter Orlovsky
died yesterday. Remembering those who died in war
and those who lived their lives in service of art and peace.

The honeysuckle by my porch sends up pale pink fingers
 to a mushy sky while fuchsia bells wear their elegance
in a head bowed demeanor. A songbird sings a song

I don't recognize or understand. And the dishes sit
in the sink unfinished and unembarrassed. Chocolate
cake half-eaten drowns on a soggy plate.

And the fuchsia colored dahlia is ready
to explode. "Of asphodel that greeny flower," shouts
Williams. Green, green, green he screams.

A squirrel screams and reminds me of the monkeys in Nepal.
The ceramic Buddha on my porch holds his hand out so I
place shells, rocks and bits of glass into his ceramic hand.

And yet the dishes, yes the dishes remain unfinished as I listen
to the songbirds tell me winter is over. Yes, and summer is
beginning. Yes, yes, yes.

Memory is elusive. "Of asphodel that greeny flower,"
The rhythm of warblers, the rhythm of the shiny creek
versus the hard creek, versus the tumbling creek, the tumbling.

Seirks creek rumbles past with salmon fry that were hatched
last fall, ready to begin their lives in the creeks and rivers
and oceans of the world. Memorial Day—fuchsia,
honeysuckle, plum and green. Rivers rumble, tumble by.

WE KICKED THEM OUT OF PARADISE

When we get to the tomb of Old Chief Joseph
the sky turns dark and thunder cracks.
We have traveled through the *Nimiipuum Wetes*
the Nez Perce Homeland. *Nimiipuum*: The people.

The sky turns dark and thunder cracks.
The white men thought they were nomads.
The Nez Pierce Homeland. *Nimiipuum*: The people.
They lived in the high valleys in summer.

The white men thought we were nomads.
We lived deep in the canyons in winter.
We lived in the high valley in summer.
The lake is a ghost of the glacier.

We lived deep in the canyons in winter.
Pleistocene glaciers formed the lake.
The lake is a ghost of the glacier.
Our women dug roots in early spring.

Pleistocene glaciers formed the lake.
Our men fished for Salmon-wáts'ya.
Our women picked berries in summer.
Wetes: sacred, ha'wtnin' supernatural power.

The men fished for Salmon-núsux.
The invisible laws (tamalwit), sought by the people.
Wetes: sacred, ha'wtnin' supernatural power
the birds, fish, mammals, insects are rightful owners.

The invisible laws (*tamalwit*), sought by the people.
Other travelers have placed: aluminum flowers.
The birds, fish, mammals, insects are rightful owners.
Dimes and nickels, the ace of diamonds.

Other travelers have placed: aluminum flowers.
I don't much believe in spirits.

Dimes and nickels, the ace of diamonds.
There are ghosts dancing here.

I don't much believe in spirits.
A Ponderosa has been struck by lightning
There are ghosts dancing here.
A river rattles on the other side.

A Ponderosa has been struck by lightning
Its reddish trunk scarred and twisted
A river rattles on the other side.
Some kind of white fur litters these hills.

Its reddish trunk scared and twisted.
I place tobacco from my American Spirit.
Some kind of white fur litters these hills.
The sky turns darker and I weep.

I place tobacco from my American Spirit
a flash, another crack and the skies open.
The sky turns darker and I weep.
We kicked them out of paradise.

BIG FROG CLAN

1. Doris's grandson was quite ill, and fell into a deep coma.
   He dreamt of a lake so blue and clear. Amongst the grey

   and green shimmering rocks, at the bottom of the lake
   he could see the faces of the ancestors. He remembered

   these faces—aunties and uncles, cousins and great-grandparents.
   They told him a great evil was coming. They told him

   PROTECT THE LAKE. The doctors thought
   he might not make it, but the man awoke

   and knew the lake was Morristown Lake, fed by
   pristine waters of the *Whedzin Kwah*, a lake so pure

   you can dip your cup into it and drink. *The ancestors are here.*

2. Chevron, Enbridge and TransCanada want to drill
   under Morristown Lake. The *Unist'ot'en* people

   have taken a stand, built a healing lodge and
   pit house in the path of the bulldozers. Erected

   a blockade at the bridge that spans the *Wedzin Kwah*—
   a border crossing onto unceded *Unist'ot'en* land.

   They have held the oil companies at bay, companies that want
   to hurl tar sands and fracked oil swooshing under Morristown Lake.

   The rest of the *Wet'suwet'en* people have heeded the call,
   built their own blockades. The RCMP by order of the federal

   and provincial government are planning to breech the blockades
   of the *Wet'suweten* people. *The ancestors are here.*

3. You are walking on the road by yourself at dusk, gravel
   and dry pine branches crunching below your feet.

You are not alone. When you think a mama bear and cub
might be staring you down from the brush *You are not alone.*

When you see a black figure at the end of a logging road
and think it might be a bear, but comes closer and wags

her tail. *You are not alone.* When the nighthawk *Mintz'eth*
calls at dusk, *You are not alone.* The wind sweeps down

from snow-capped *Dzilh Yez*, shakes the pine boughs,
and whispers *You are not alone.* The moon rises full

like a bronze-colored looney. At midnight, the moose's
giant antlers are in shadow. The raven circles

searching for beaver entrails. *You are not alone.*

THE CHIEFS

After a night in Prince George, then miles of swerving
logging roads, my husband and I arrive at the bridge
that crosses the Wedsen Khah. We are greeted by a scraggly-
haired kid who grunts into a crackling walkie-talkie.
Three people wearing down coats, fur hats pulled low
over their eyebrows, descend from the Healing Centre
we are there to help build.

To cross the border onto unceded Wesuiten land
we must answer a series of questions:
Have you ever worked for a major oil company?
Do you intend us any harm?
What skills do you bring?
How can you assist our people in this struggle?

After five days of spackling, calking and defrosting
lynx and beaver meat, we have the opportunity to meet
the chiefs. Chief Nedabis is the oldest, sips a McCafe,
as he warms himself by the wood stove. *The roads
are like pea soup*, he warns, *had trouble even in my new Toyoto*.

Chief Doris is the spitting image of my husband's
German grandmother. Doris is patient with me
as I try to pronounce Smogilhgim, the hereditary name
for the Chief of the Sun House of the Fireweed Clan.
Trying to speak the language is like rolling river rocks
around in my mouth. Smogilhgim just glares at me.

Helen is the quietest chief. I accidently get her in the frame
as I take a picture of my friend Lisa skinning a martin. Helen
says it is okay as long as I show her the picture. She nods
in approval. Both she and Lisa are wearing red.

.

When I pass him on my way to the outhouse, Chief Nedabis
tells me *Watch out for Grizzlies. They like white meat.*
I laugh and tell him I have only seen black bear.

HOW I LEARNED TO LOVE THE MOURNING DOVE AGAIN

I. JUNE

Sometimes, I want it all to stop. This incessant
quarrelling of the red-brown fox squirrel, the croaking

of the lime-green tree frog, the twittering
of the song sparrows, it is too much.

The peck-pecking of the red-headed woodpecker,
the honking of the Sandhill cranes flying south, their feet

dangling beneath them in the peach-colored sky.
I want it all to stop. Especially, this wailing

of the pastel-colored mourning dove.

II. JULY

For years, I wanted to live where I could wake to the mourning dove.
This spring when a dove moved into our Oregon neighborhood

she drove me crazy with her incessant keening. Now, I wake
to her sweet and sour sound in West Branch, Iowa, in Chicago,

in Slidell, Louisiana. I drink hot coffee with chicory as birds steal figs
from a tree, not minding the shiny CDs meant to ward them off.

I smell rosemary. Last night in Baton Rouge, Alton Sterling
was shot by police in the chest at point-blank range for selling CDs.

He was wearing a red shirt. In Minnesota, Philando Castile is stopped
for a broken tail light. He tells the officers he has a license to carry.

They tell him to raise his hands. They tell him to get his license
and registration. They shoot him in front of his girlfriend and child.

In the video, his little girl tells him *It is okay, I am here with you.*

III. JANUARY

In the middle of January, I hear the mourning dove.
She says *You must write this, you must write this!*

A white supremacist raises his glass and shouts,
"Hail Trump. Hail our People! Hail victory!"

In White Fish, Montana, a Neo-Nazi group
plans an armed march through the center of town

The trolls rail against the Jewish citizens
of White Fish, "You would all be of greater worth

…as human fertilizer." someone writes on Facebook.
At home in Oregon, I recite the Kaddish, as I light the candles.

*Baruch atah, Adanois Eloheinu, Melech haolam, asher kid'shanu
b'mitsvatav v'tsiaanu l'hadlik ner shel Hannukka.*

In Whitefish the sun rises on January 20th, and the morning
light splinters into a thousand pieces on the frozen sidewalk.

A flyer with Auchwitz, and the face of Rabbi Secher blows
down the deserted street, and paper menorahs cover the *Wall of Peace*.

The Neo-Nazi march was cancelled. A small group of protesters
serve Matzo ball soup, and chant *Love not Hate*.

IV. JUNE

This morning the dove sounds angrier, louder,
more insistent. Her shrieking is as irritating

as the cloying smell of the feral honeysuckle
flourishing along the fence. Green, this

uncompromising rain has encouraged too much
green. Outside the window the flag is at half-mast.

On a commuter train in Portland, Oregon, a man
appears out of nowhere and begins hurling racial slurs

at two African-American girls. One wears a hijab.
Three bystanders on the train come to the rescue.

Ricky John Best, Taliesen Myrddin Namkaai-Mechee,
and Micah David Cole Fletcher are stabbed by this

Neo-nazi. Only Fletcher survives. He speaks from his hospital bed,
an angry crimson scar snaking from his left ear down his chest.

He tells the reporter *Imagine for a second—being that little
girl on the MAX. This man is screaming at you, his face a pile*

*of knives, his body is a gun. Everything is cocked, loaded and ready
to kill you."* The killer's last name is Christian. A video shot in April

shows Christian standing in a Burger King parking lot wrapped
in a pre-Revolutionary War flag. He casts a Nazi salute

and shouts, "Die Muslims!" When arraigned, Christian yells,
"Get out if you don't like free speech…You call it terrorism;

I call it patriotism You hear me? Die." In Oregon two men are killed,
and one is injured for doing the right thing. I hear the mourning dove.

She tells me *You must write this! You must write this!*

JESÚS AND THE COLORED PENCILS

A Pantoum

My student's brother was killed today, shot, and left for dead.
Jesús fled cartel violence, stays in his cell and screams.
I want to give my students bear hugs, but this is not allowed.
He screams and screams. I can't imagine the things he's seen.

Jesús has fled cartel violence. Stays in his cell and screams.
Juan remembers the blood streaming onto the sidewalk.
He screams and screams. I can't imagine the things he's seen.
He was eight. The man was stabbed in the neck.

Juan remembers the blood streaming onto the sidewalk
in Honduras as he left with his mother. She abandoned him.
He was eight. The man had been stabbed in the neck.
José tells me he is a cold-blooded killer *Yes it is true.*

In Honduras as he left with his mother. She abandoned him.
José is fifteen: short and cute. Grins slyly.
José tells me he is a cold-blooded killer *Yes it is true.*
Brendan is back for the tenth time; we are like family to him.

José is fifteen: short and cute. Grins slyly.
That kid doesn't understand we are killers in here.
Brendan is back for the tenth time; we are like family to him.
The kid is only eleven, what did he do?

That kid doesn't understand we are killers in here.
He likes Zombie comics and Sponge Bob.
The kid is only eleven, what did he do?
Power Rangers, Star Wars and coloring books.

He likes Zombie comics and Sponge Bob.
My student's brother was shot in a park.
Power Rangers, Star Wars and coloring books.
Portland, Oregon: 503 Boys, Blood or Crips?

My student's brother was shot in a park.
In the classroom Jesús requests colored pencils.
Portland, Oregon: 503 Boys, Blood or Crips?
He wants to color between the lines—a Corvette.

In the classroom Jesús requests colored pencils
He wants a black, a cherry red, a sky blue.
He wants to color between the lines—a Corvette.
He wants to color his dream, but that is not allowed.

He wants a black, a cherry red, a sky blue.
You could stab a person in the neck with a pencil.
He wants to color his dream, but that is not allowed.
How many lives and dreams have we cancelled?

You could stab a person in the neck with a pencil.
My student's brother was killed today, shot, and left for dead.
How many lives and dreams have we cancelled?
I want to give my students bear hugs, but this is not allowed.

INFERNO

This is the summer of flashbangs and teargas swirling pink through the streets. Angry rants on Facebook. *You go ahead and try your insurrection or race war or whatever else you have in mind. It will be the last thing you attempt. LOSER.* Nazis, White Supremacists, Patriot Prayer and Proud Boys. The Alt Right claims a "freedom march." Communists, Socialists, Antifi. *Say the whole word—MFO—Antifascists.* This is the summer of pierced helmets. This is the summer of Joey Gibson saying he will cleanse Portland of the angry welts of disappointment. Starbucks won't bother opening. This is the summer of almost the mid-terms. If we don't flip were fucked. This is the summer of flip-flops called thongs, called zoris, flip-flopping over the asphalt as heat waves rise up and slap us in the face. Hottest year on record. Again. *We are making history, baby.* California erupting in fireballs and fire tornados. At sunrise an angry red disk rises in the Eastern sky. Smoke is snagged in raggedy firs. Smoke from California. Last year it was Canada. Fucking Canada and we live in Oregon. It smelled like smoke every day in August and September. Ash rained down like snow on cars and trucks. This is the summer of gnarled dead trees on the ridges as I drive up the Gorge. This is the summer of warty Patty Pan squash, tendrils lengthening and spiraling around cabbage, cauliflower and amaranth. This is the summer of alternate reality turning into out-right lies. This is the summer of tent-caterpillars hanging from the cottonwoods and alders and raspberry leaves withering in the heat. This is the summer of hungry bees, log trucks roaring by on the 30 blowing air horns, yellow jackets careening around the hose bib, stinging my knuckle, my hand swelling to the size of a cantaloupe, a cantaloupe I can't eat because my throat will swell. This is the summer of spider webs dangling from every tomato plant, spiders in my hair, on my face. This is the summer of the brown recluse bite blistering, pussing, and bursting open.

A SLENDER THREAD

> *...he is somewhere on the periphery, whirling like a whirligig, going faster and faster and blinder and blinder.*
> Henry Miller

Above the dark green Jacuzzi pool, a leaf whirls and twirls, going faster and faster hanging from a slender thread. A spider thread? Everyone in the pool watches as a squirrel scurries over a metal fence and through the brush, knocking into the thread. The leaf wobbles, slows, then almost stops. Finally, after what seems like an eternity, the leaf resumes its whirling. She wants another drink. Orange hair. The top of a Dawn Redwood sways as the wind picks up. The leaf whirls and twirls, going faster and faster.

A slender thread is all that ties me to a reality full of holes. If you add very hot coffee to soymilk, the soy clumps into a gooey mass that floats just under the black coffee on this steaming June morning with the sprinklers whirring and the china clattering in the main dining room. The gooey mass will dissipate with stirring, and constant vigilance which does not allow me to notice that the American flag is at three-quarters mast. Someone in the US is shot dead every fifteen minutes.

On the porch of the Grand Lodge hotel, as I read Henry Miller's *Wisdom of the Heart*, a middle-aged man in a tan shirt and brown shorts drinks coffee from a paper cup. He faces a red brick wall, then rises and turns to face the brimming blue sky, the scarlet roses and purple Lupine, orange shooting-star lilies and native Columbine that give way to manicured lawns that stretch to furrowed fields. The smell of fennel.

New cup of Joe. Steamed soy so it doesn't curdle. Such a slender thread. Red roses are clinging to everything. Roses don't really cling, since they have nothing to grab onto, but send out long canes to be trained. The leaf is still twirling. Open your eyes. Don't become blind. Am I the whirligig going faster and blinder, or am I the squirrel that disrupts the whole works.

HOME

HOME

Car rattle, cat squeak
Screen door slam, creek rumble
Fly buzz, chicken babble
Bird twitter, human ramble

Saw screech, raven caw.
The frog that has been silent
since spring erupts.

On a bit of lily, three frogs
Just bigger than grains of rice.
Brown and green.

THIS

is all there is. This
sopping
weather, this croaking river,
this curse of succulent.
Tomatoes, bright red
and green, amaranth,
sucking
mouth. Ripe. Too much
to do. This is all there is.
White grape groping
for plum and impressed
by nothing
climbs higher than it
should
ever be allowed to. This
is all there is: this curve
of succulent, the way
the Hopi Red amaranth
bends
its brilliant head.

AS EACH

moment follows the last
one after the other like rain drops,
the path follows the shore.
Beach grass bunched in hollows
stings when you brush past.
My father lived his whole life
in colder climes.
Rain falls sideways in winter
and whiteouts are common.
No sense brooding about the past.
At times my tongue is plastered
to the roof of my mouth
like I forgot to wash the toothpaste out.
I sweat salty tears, am hot then cold,
hung over, though
I have sipped
only water.

Imagine summer:
the taste of tomatoes, the leafy smell
when you brush past.
The white jasmine
planted in the ceramic pot,
the tulips crowning
on the bank
of Seirks Creek
where salmon spawn.

ANT SEX

When I grab my journal off the picnic table
two carpenter ants are fighting
curled
in a death dance—
legs flailing, searching each other's
bodies.
They roll, bounce, separate, roll back
together.
Three body segments, then six
are bound together
rolling.
Pearlescent black bands
encircle
their stinger sections.
They roll
writhe
separate
come back together.
Then,
it is over.
One ant saunters
away.
The other
patiently sifts
through a pile
of earth.

IS THE BUDDHA SPEAKING?

The Buddha sits on my front porch.
A ceramic statue,
he wears cracked blue robes
and stares with dragonfly-colored eyes.
He holds his hand out
for offerings.
I occasionally place a sparkling pebble,
or a bit of moss
in his outstretched palm.

For the last month
or so
every so often,
but you never know
when:
ribbit, ribbit.

I pick up the Buddha
shake him
look under the bowl of rocks
next to him
search the wisteria
trained over the porch,
the withering honeysuckle.
I pick up every little bit
of flotsam and jetsam
that has landed on this porch,
and NOTHING.

Just when I think
he has stopped speaking
I hear,
ribbit, ribbit!

PLUM

Rooster crows at the break of…
Brilliant primrose and stunning
Proud rosemary adorn the newly scrubbed
porch. The creek—a true alto—sings
a song and above it all plums.
I dream of ripe plums blazing into glory
despite the plummeting thermometer.
Fuchsia, verdant green, robin-egg
blue, mid-morning sky.

THE STRUGGLE

The arborvitae is tipped with frost
and the plum struggles to bloom,
a sickly white. In the distance
a wild cherry is licked by sunlight,
and in the garden the snow pea
shoots timidly lift their tiny heads.
The bamboo is littered with dew
and the frog emits a tenuous croak.

CARNIVORE

1.

Today I watched my cat eat a whole baby rat. She wanted
to bring it inside, but I shoo her out to eat it on the dewy
grass. Usually I don't see her eat her kills, only see some blood
and a few entrails: a stomach, a liver, a kidney, but today
I saw the blood drip out of her mouth as she swallowed
the head and chomped down on the spine. Watched
as the tail hung out of her mouth then disappeared.
All that was left was a kidney glistening in the sun.

2.

As you walk into the garden you see the first one lying supine,
the white fur on its gray belly is moist and mottled. I turn away
in disgust, then make myself turn and watch the carnage.
Two little white teeth jut out like pearls. Rigor mortis. Four gray
paws stick straight up into the blue air. Then you see the next one
in a patch of sun next to the Snowberry plant. A full grown Norway
Rat on its back, minus its head. The belly expertly ripped open
exposing spleen, liver, kidney, heart. 15 or 20 baby yellow jackets
buzz and chew and push each other out of the way for a chance
to gorge on the glistening entrails, and I think of Anthony Bourdain,
how he loved the organ meats grilled over an open flame.

ROOSTER (A PANTOUM)

You stand tall in the morning sun, your red comb glistens
In the morning sun. Your red comb high on your stupendous
Head. The lawn mower whines, the creek rumbles listen
To the sounds of this glorious morning, look around you on this

In the morning sun. Your red comb high on your stupendous
You and Bessie search for grubs in the glittering grass, search
To the sounds of this glorious, look around you this
Incredible morning. You and Bessie plop down beside me search

You and Bessie search for grubs in the glittering grass, search
For mites in your speckled brown side. Your tail feathers inky black
On this incredible morning you and Bessie plop down beside me search
Your tail feathers an inky blue green, search for mites on your back

For mites in your speckled brown side, your tail feathers an inky
Fluorescent blue turning to fluorescent green. For what do you search?
Your tail feathers an inky blue green, search for mites on your back
What do you see when you turn your stupendous red head, search?

Fluorescent blue turning to fluorescent green. What do you search
For in the glittering grass, what do you see? That bright orange.
What do you see when you turn your stupendous red head search
That bright orange eye stares at me and asks me something strange

You stand tall in the morning sun, your red comb glistens
Incredible head. The lawn mower whines, the creek rumbles listen.

SALMON SPAWNING SUNDAY

Maple leaves drop like Sasquatch
prints around solid firs and spindly
snags. Fog spreads an eerie form.
It's been raining for days.

Then, the sun emerges
a faint disk in the southern sky. Suddenly,
a pair of Coho—only dark shapes
at first—a little riffle, a splash, then a fin,
a fluorescent scaly side.

Back and forth they dance, rise up,
sink, ready gravel and soft mud.
Then a splashing so violent
it muddies the water to a froth.

You see the bruised moth-eaten
skin scraped raw, oozing red.

We are all going home to a still place
surrounded by sleeping cedar with verdant
fingers sweeping the surface of a dark pool.
Lacy alder dancing.

WITHERED

Bitter cold. Coffee.
Wisteria bean pods hang down.
Like withered testes

POEMS
IN THE KEY
OF SEA

HIGHWAY 30

mirrors the Columbia
        on its way to the Pacific.
                Shed roof
                        blue building.
Topless has become
                To Bless.
Sign on Lundberg's Grocery
                Tanning
                      Toning
                            Saw Sharpening.
Where nuclear power
                        plant once stood
                                  vultures.

HOOD CANAL

The empty metal rowboats
sway wily-nilly at anchor
in a sea that can only be called
ultra-marine. The grandchildren
spot a seal bobbing a little further out.
At the end of the pier
my sister, brother and I
hoist the now half-full bag
quickly dump the white ashes
which float on the blue-green
surface
for just a moment
then swirl, sink
disappear.

WILLAPA BAY, BEGINNING OF JUNE

No see-ums can you see them? Calm.
Can you hear the ocean five miles away?
Screeching woke me. A child? What's wrong?

Merely diving-terns. Come on.
Seals. Is there salmon in this bay?
I hold a periwinkle in my palm.

One branch rubs against another, morning song.
Tides out, the sky a gentle gray.
Tides out, children move along.

Skyscape reminds me of Thailand, Vietnam.
We thought Cow Parsnip was Ocean Spray.
Thunderheads gather on the horizon.

A touch of sun on jade hills, a psalm
An errant thought, a single ray
We can wonder, wander with such aplomb.

If we try, these cedars become palms.
In these temperate winds they sway.
My nerves so frayed are calm.
When I breathe here, nothing's wrong.

WILLAPA BAY, END OF AUGUST

*What looks like sixteen
men stooped on the spit is really
piles of fresh oysters.*

When I was five we walked hand
in hand here, my father and I.
He told me that these mud flats
stretch all the way to China.
Now, he can't remember
saying that or how to go
to the bathroom. I remember:

a bucket of clams on the porch
of the cabin we were staying in,
the clams soaking in salt water
so they would spit out all the sand,
sometimes getting spit on,
tanning on the beach on a striped beach
towel, my dad's hairy back and chest.
He used to say
he had more hair on his body
than his head.

Now, I hold his hand as we listen
to Big Band music and sometimes
he can't remember my name.

*Ten seagulls like old men
waddle over the mud flats
searching for what?*

MERROIR/EATING RAW OYSTERS IS LIKE EATING THE OCEAN

The first time David took me to Willapa, we departed the dock
as the tide was sucked out to sea. Stuck in a narrow channel
unable to turn the kayak around, we jumped into knee-deep water
and slurped raw oysters as the rain dripped off our hats onto our necks
until the tide reversed, knowing full well that oysters are an aphrodisiac.

When I was growing up, my mother cooked oysters every Friday—
coated in egg and fried in butter. These oysters usually came
from a jar bought at the grocery. *The word Merroir was coined
by oyster farmers. Mer (sea) + terroir—the salt water elements
found in the sea or river… that contribute to the distinctive taste…*

At Tomales Bay, I kayak across a channel to an oyster
farm, buy two bags worth. I can't eat them anymore,
but watch enviously as the boys grill them in the shell
on the rim of the fire pit, then pop the steaming oysters
into their mouths. A bobcat watches, hidden in the brush.

Now, we cook them this way at Willapa, but if I could eat them
I would stand in the rain in a knee-deep ocean with water dripping
down my neck, shucking and slurping oysters one by one
as the ocean recedes, and the sun becomes a burnt copper disk
sliding through clouds the color of an ancient nickel.

WHEN I CAME TO THE DESERT I DIDN'T THINK I WOULD WRITE A POEM ABOUT THE SEA

but in Death Valley, a plant with succulent green
and pink shoots grows right out of the salt flat.
This must be the same plant we forage in the shallows
of Willapa Bay. One bite produces on my tongue
a burst of salt. Salicornia known as Pickleweed.
Sun reflecting off the flats burns my eyes. White
salt flat and water stretch towards snow-capped
mountains and mountains are reflected back.
Five million years ago marine animals
thrived here in a warm shallow sea.

MONOGAMOUS

At dusk two white geese
      float in ink dark water
           swim as a pair.

White against dark create
      shimmering V's
           as a they swim.

Clouds drift apart.
      Full white moon.
           A circle of white.

At dusk two white geese
      swim as a pair,
           eat granola from my hand.

Two white geese swim
      In gentle green circles.
           A white duck follows.

For years, two white geese
      swimming in gentle circles
           a white duck following.

A clatter of migrating geese
      rise up into dark trees.
           Boom, boom, boom.

Last night at dusk—
      a single white goose
           floats in ink dark water.

Last night at dusk—
      A single white goose
           his honks echoing off
                  the dark and brooding banks.

ALL THE SADNESS

wells up and spills over boulders.
Breathe cedar and granite. Snow
rests in crevices before cascading into
horsetail falls, then over gray cliffs
into valleys exploding with wild rose.

I write as rain falls over the sea, and sea
otters float by laughing and munching
on clams placed on their fat bellies.
Ravens knock and whales dive far under
where we believe the surface to be.

Moss thickens on knots and burls of cedar
and hemlock. The sound on the tent is like someone
opening cellophane to get to the green jelly candy inside.

Rainwater fills up the granite basins where She-bear
pisses to insure that only the initiated will drink.
And occasionally when the sky lightens and the sun
emerges from his hiding place among billowing clouds,
the wild roses are blanketed with diamonds.

POEM WRITTEN AFTER READING STEVENS AND NIEDECKER AND TRYING TO QUIT COFFEE

End of earth
        gray ocean
                rolls towards my heart

and out. Man gazes
        towards rolling.
                Hat in hand.

A single pelican
        floats, rises
                outstretched

wings cover air
        water. I want
                coffee.

Little shore
        birds twitter forward
                backward fill the air

with music. How do I write
        this? Start
                with object.

Is it rock or shell?
        Once held
                something with cells

that divided,
        now wears
                a skirt of pleated pink.

Breakers crash
        leave smooth gray
                and brown sand

where I walk

   with bare feet.
     Tracks

are soon
   washed away.
      Ocean rolls.

I want coffee.
   Wild fennel bends
      this way and that

fractures gray
   with yellow.
      Waves break.

I walk through
   wild rosemary
      poison oak.

Graffiti shouts
   AWAKEN!

DON'T TURN YOUR BACK ON THE OCEAN

North of Eureka, we meet Jack, a blonde-haired surfer from Australia. *What types of waves are best for surfing?* I ask. *Rollers that steepen up way out, have a nice open face.* I tell him about the Olympic Sport of Wave Watching. I am looking for similar waves, but not quite. In *my* sport you find a spot on the beach, or on a cliff where you can see the ocean. A cup of coffee is nice. You look towards the horizon, pick one wave and follow it with your gaze as long as possible. You might see it foam, crest and join its mate and then another. If it is windy the top of the wave might get blown off like a party streamer. And then closer to shore you might see a whole community of waves crash and tumble white and frothy like the inside of a front-loading washing machine. Closer in yet, you might notice as the wave recedes—a crosshatch pattern made by the wind skimming the surface of the water. Then you start over. Pick another wave as far out as you can see. It is legal to stand as long as you don't lose your focus. The object is to stay in one spot as long as possible. Maybe it is warm, and you are barefoot. Feel the suck as your toes sink into the sand. Notice how the sky changes from dark gray, to white, to cobalt blue. Remember to breathe in and out. Here on this crescent beach, notice the waves roll in and spread out like white lace on black sand.

NO WORD FOR WANT

After the 2004 Indian Ocean earthquake and tsunami,
a total of 250, 000 people died, but all of the native people
of the Simian Islands, the Sea Gypsies, survived.

Pennant Fish, Parrot Fish, Emperor Angel. Rising
sea temperatures bleach the coral white. Electric
greens, brilliant blues, the black and yellow of Coral Fish.

Table coral, Galaxy coral, Coral Brain.
Fat white tourists redden as they float
on their bellies. Gawk at these bright fish.

Sea Gypsies—Morgan, Mogen, Moken all are correct.
Means *Immersed in Water.* During the Bronze Age
they were pushed to the sea by less-peace-loving peoples.

Now, they inhabit 800 islands in the Andaman Sea.
A Moken man moves through water like a hungry shark,
plunging under coral boulders to take lobster.

I don't see any people as I step off the boat
into the turquoise water. Behind a row of bamboo huts,
a row of brightly dressed women and girls display their wares.

She smiles as she hands me the necklace—plastic,
the blue-green color of a Parrot Fish. The white
goo on her face protects from the sun.

The men are as dark as mahogany.
She was younger then, but knew just what to do.
Gather the children and run for higher ground.

Laboons occur every 800 years. Government records go back
only 700. The ancestors had been warning for weeks: deep sea fish
appeared near the surface. Hermit crabs scuttled into the forest.

*Jok was the headman's son. His dead brother came to him in a dream
Told him to warn the people, tell them to go to higher ground.
But Jok had to go to work, take tourists snorkeling.*

*He could not stop shaking. Something was wrong. "Maybe too much coffee."
Suddenly, all the boats were grounded, but it was high tide. The Laboon!
Jok saved many people, but some tourists were too dumb to listen.*

*As headman, Selamat assumed his duty and stood with arms raised
confronting the oncoming wave. "Laboon, do not be strong!"
he yelled, "Spare our village." But the first wave knocked him down.*

*The women and children ran to higher ground. Selamet clutched a pillar
of a house, but knew the next wave would take him. He ran up the hill
to join the rest. A head count revealed that all had survived.*

The government relocated the Moken to the mainland, but they
didn't like it there. Without the government's knowledge, they
snuck back to the island, and rebuilt the village within a few months.

The Moken have no word for "want" because the sea provides
everything they need. After the *Laboon*, when asked what they
"wanted," they requested a drum, so they could dance and sing.

I pick a bracelet from the gap-toothed woman. She does not
need teeth to spit out bones. I pick an orange and black
geometric design like the drum they played to give thanks
to the ancestors who allowed them to survive.

RUBBER TREES

Rows of rubber trees like alder. Black metal cups attached to the trunk catch white sap. It turns black like opium. What are those things that look like pinecones? Bananas? In the palm oil plantation dappled light. Trespassing. I walk up the dung-covered path. Cloudy eye of elephant means cataracts. Two dark-haired children walk home from school, uniform shirts starched white. Dark pants/skirt. *Sowadi kah. Khun Chua a-rai.* Good day. What is your name? Plumeria. Pink cups. The elephants knew the Tsunami was coming, lumbered to higher ground. Rainstorm. Tukah tukah. Little gecko. I can't stop crying.

Jungle sings. Rain drips off bamboo hut. Girls ride motorbikes wearing red lipstick and high heels. Roosters crow. Monkeys maybe. Mama pig and all her piglets. Kratom leaves are a stimulant related to the coffee plant used by fishermen for years to cool off. Chew too much and your heart will stop. Too much betel nut will turn your mouth bright red. White stork-like bird soars, lands on the back of a lone cow to pick off bugs. The sky lightens revealing swaying palms. I can't stop crying.

Jump in the Andaman
Sea at sunset. Swim in salty waves.
Float. Breathe.

VENUS DISAPPEARING

Corner of paradise, cedar-shaked building the white arbor
and picket fence. Ocean turning from black to cobalt to white
waves crashing and the sound, the never ending
                          crashing.

Dream—the room is shaking *The Big One* You are supposed
to run, but I can't run. Everything moving. The walls are closing in.
Much less disturbing than the re-occurring dream of trying to
                          conceive

though I am eight years past menopause. Wake to find
I am in a room by the ocean. Sound of the world coming
to me, sound of my heart. Venus
                          disappearing.

The sky turns from cobalt to gray to light blue, then shell-pink.
Last evening a line of bodies, dark against shimmering sand
moving like ants. Tide way out. Were they dreaming of
                          clams?

Driving to the coast on a Friday evening through massive
trees, through winding traffic and patches of white snow.
Everyone driving to the coast on a Friday in
                          January.

We park our cars and stride to the edge of the ocean to look out
and contemplate our little difficulties. On the edge of the world
waves keep crashing never stop crashing huge and white on dark
                          sand.

The next morning if you are patient, as you sip your coffee
you will see the moment the sea goes from a dark brooding mass
to gray to white waves crashing against tan and you will see Venus

                          disappear.

TWISTED LITTLE LOVE SONGS

FLAME

Travelling with Ben away from the reunion. West Branch Iowa to Chicago. Scotty in the back seat. Stop for coffee at a gas station/convenience/ tourist and trinket shop with a Starbucks. Ben flirts with the girl at the counter, tells her I was his girlfriend 30 years ago. Treats me like a queen. Fireworks crackle in the humid air even though it is only the third of July. The sales girl tells us this is a tradition in Illinois She wishes she could come with us. We get back in the car with our steaming coffees, reliving that feeling of first love even though I was 31 then, and already had been married and divorced. I had never felt that crushing exuberance and devastation of first love. I tell Ben how devastated I was back then when he slept with that other woman in New York City, and all I wanted to do was jump onto the subway tracks, onto the third rail and end it all. I can't remember the joke, but I am laughing so hard I think I am going to spill my coffee. Laughing so hard that I am finally crying. I tell Ben I can't cry in a crowd, and he reminds me of all those times I called from that distant and isolated phone booth in rural Vermont with the winter stars and the waning moon mocking me and the dirty frozen snow crunching under my feet, and crying and crying unwilling to hang up.

GEM # 3 BEAUTIFUL SOUL

Honking and echoes in this underground chamber. It is not as warm as I thought, and I shiver in my sleeveless blouse. I am overwhelmed by a long line of yellow taxis. A guy gets out, and puts my luggage in the trunk. *We're close. With this traffic I don't know.* He speaks with a lilting African accent. *Really it is only 15/20 minutes without traffic, but it is rush hour. Forty-five minutes maybe an hour. You have a beautiful soul. I can tell.* We weave in and out of traffic. A lot more honking. Cars pull out into the intersection at most every cross street, and we have to swerve into the oncoming lane to get around them. *Traffic in Chicago, you get used to it.* We pass Korean markets, Mexican pastry shops, Russian gift shops. Emmanuel moved from Nigeria to London before the civil war. In London, he received a degree in Molecular Biology. *As a cabbie, I am my own man, can do what I want.* He has two grown daughters, one is a CPA, the other a lawyer. They live in Africa with his ex-wife. *Man falls in love and will do anything for the woman, buy her flowers, follow her anywhere, but the woman is more practical, makes sure the man has a good job, can provide for her. Men are just little boys, vying for attention.* Traffic has stalled on this two-lane city street. There is no traffic in the other lane, so Emmanuel swerves into that lane, and drives half a block Going The Wrong Way to negotiate a left turn onto a side street, goes around a couple blocks. And we are there. He pulls my luggage out of the trunk; we part with a handshake. He tells me again *You have a beautiful soul. I can tell.*

GEM #4 ETTA ON THE CITY OF NEW ORLEANS

I squeeze my way down the narrow aisle to find my seat. 53B. An older black woman sits in the window seat. She wipes the seatback and the arm rests with a Clorox wipe, then hands me one. Offers me a package of pre-popped popcorn which I stuff into the seatback pocket. We are on the City of New Orleans, waiting to leave the Chicago station. Etta is going to visit her 91-year-old mother in Mississippi. I am going to the end-of-the-line. New Orleans. We are both retired school teachers. Etta brought the rest of her lunch—sour smelling pickled hot chilies. I eat of my sausage and mozzarella sub. It is 8pm on the Fourth of July. As we wend our way through the southernmost burbs of Chicago, Etta points to a white burst of sparkles in the bruised sky. Fireworks. The train whistle blows.

By 9 pm most of the passengers—including Etta—are asleep, wrapped in blankets or coats, or extra clothing. As the train chugs and sways through the dark, I find the lyrics to Steve Goodman's *City of New Orleans* on my phone and softly hum along: *Dealin' cards with the old men in the club car/Penny a point ain't no one keepin' score/Won't you pass the paper bag that holds the bottle/Feel the wheels rumblin' 'neath the floor.*

Travelers wake and stumble towards coffee on the stalled train. I order mine black. Chet, the service attendant sounds like he is growling, but it is only his Cajun accent. Chet and myself are the only white people in this car. I spend the remainder of the morning in the lounge drinking coffee; pink crepe myrtle is brilliant against the verdant landscape. The conductor calls out *Clarksdale, Marvel, Elaine*. The train chugs, and swerves, slows down, speeds up, goes faster and switches tracks. *Phillips County; Black Bayou; Brookhaven; Greenwood, Mississippi*. We must be getting close to Etta's stop. I head back to my seat thinking I might eat that popcorn now, but is no longer in the seatback pocket. I drop into my seat; Etta reaches into her purse and pulls out the popcorn. *I thought you didn't want it.*

GEM #5 GREG

Behind the columns in front of the St. Louis Cathedral I find enough shade to finish my cappuccino. The guy I met yesterday, Greg, is there with his white tuba slathered with stickers: Naked, LSU and a fluer-de-lis. There are eight other guys with horns, trombones, trumpets. I snap a couple of pictures. Then a guy with a trombone runs over pointing to my camera. *What*? I ask, *Do you want my camera?* He wants to take a picture of me with the band. I sit next to the trumpet player. The trombone guy comes back. *It says, No Battery.*

Oh, well. I sit on that bench in the direct noonday sun; sip my cappuccino. The guy with the trumpet wearing a ripped brown t-shirt over his protruding gut stands up and begins to sing sounding just like Louis Armstrong.

GEM #6 STERLING @ ANTOINE'S IN THE FRENCH QUARTER

Antoine's is the oldest family owned, continuously operated restaurant in the US. We have been advised to ask for Sterling, but there are two Sterlings—an elderly gray-haired gentleman who has worked at Antoine's his entire adult life, and Sterling Amour, who points to his name tag. *Do you know what this means?* We nod our heads in unison.

Sterling Amour is a tall black man about 40 years-old. Dozens of tables—white linen—crystal glasses. Black and white photographs and gilt-edged mirrors cover the walls. Crystal chandeliers hang above each table. Flatware clinks. You can almost hear the crinkling of chiffon petticoats as the waiters pull out the chairs to seat the *Ladies Who Lunch*. All three of us order the three course Summer Lunch Special. Sterling #1 takes are order without writing it down. He heads toward the kitchen, then turns around, *Was that two Summer Salads and one Charbroiled Oyster?*

No, one Summer Salad and two Charbroiled Oysters, we chant in unison.

Sterling #1, heads towards the kitchen, then turns around again, *Was that two Louisiana Drum Florentines and one Frenched Breast Chicken?*

Sterling Amour grins at us, *No, I have it Mr. Sterling?* They both head towards the kitchen. After lunch, which includes Lemon Cake with lemon ganache topped with raspberry drizzle, I order coffee. The coffee is very strong. I add a dollop of cream, and take a sip. I must have made a terrible face, because Sterling Amour immediately asks me what is wrong. He brings me a fresh cup of coffee, but only half full, and adds hot water until it is just the strength I prefer.

GEM #7 THE MAN IN THE RED PORK-PIE HAT

We are finishing lunch in the courtyard of Café Amelie,
with the fountain and the dragons and the stone monk
bickering about the check. The fountain drips and the
Crepe Myrtle is flowering. Thunder cracks in the white sky.
A light-skinned black man enters through the wrought iron
gate wearing a red pork-pie hat. He stands maybe five-foot-five
and wears an ivory-colored linen suit, a red tie, gold-rimmed
sunglasses. The man carries a black brief case, or maybe
it is a music case. He glides through the courtyard like a cat
stalking his prey and enters the bar. He shakes hands
with the staff. He wears white sneakers.

GEM#8 UNCLE LOUIS

A tall man in an Uncle Sam top-hat with red and blue stars and stripes and a matching tie appears to be striding into the crosswalk. The white of his tux is a stark contrast to his dark skin. His outstretched hand holds a leash attached to a battered stuffed dog about to step into traffic. I circumambulate him to see if I can detect any movement. I think I see his wrist quiver, but it might be the wind blowing the leash. After five minutes he drops the leash and grins. People clap and throw dollars into his white bucket. Everyone but me moves down the street. *I'm thirsty.* he says. Since I am thirsty too I ask him where I can buy water. He points to a shop, *They have a cooler in the front.* I buy two waters, give him one and drop a dollar in his bucket. I shake his hand, and ask him his name. *It's Uncle Louis.* His immaculate tux is ripped in the pant leg and elbow, like maybe a real dog has been chewing on it.

GEM #9 TARA IN CAMILLA'S PRODUCE

On the corner of Pontchartrain and William Tell
in Slidell, a red and green replica of a watermelon slice
hangs from an oak tree. It is cool inside. Real watermelons
are stacked on the floor, jars of something round and grey
are stacked on the mantle of a brick fireplace. Sweat drips
off my face onto the wooden floor. I wonder if it is ever cool
enough to light a fire.

I'll be out in a minute a woman's voice yells. *I'm putting up fig jam.
Figs turn so fast ya know.* I load my basket with plums, and peaches,
canned sardines, and raw peanuts.

I want to watch something else besides Zootopia. A tow-headed boy
about five-years-old peers at me from the top of a wooden
staircase. A blonde woman emerges from the back room.
Tells me I can take pictures as long as I don't sell them.

*Some tourist came in last year and took pictures and sold them
on Amazon, didn't even credit the store.* I pay for my purchases
and she hands me back some quarters. *Oh, can we trade for this one?*
Tara asks. *I give the historical ones to my kids to play with.*
On the quarter is a picture of The Drummer Boy. We trade
and I promise not to sell any of my pictures of the store on Amazon.

A LOVE LIKE THAT

Dick and Donna met in grammar school in Estacada
where farm and timber land stretch over the plains towards
Mt. Hood. Cherry trees burst into bloom, like smoke this time
of year. They have been married fifty-eight years. The doctors
incised a brain tumor out of Donna's skull, but they couldn't
get it all. She is on a restricted diet, but Dick bends his large
jean-clad body over her thin frame, feeds her the rest of his
barbecue potato chips like she is a baby bird. He wants her
to come home, but the doctors say she can't until she can keep
food down, pee on her own. Outside the hospital room,
an ornamental cherry tree bursts into full bloom.

EBU

Ebu is a phlebotomist, his nametag informs me.
He asks me where I'm from as he takes my white
arm in his large black hand. *That's where Bill Gates
lives. You rich?* "No, not at all." I tell him. Ebu ties
the blue plastic tubing around my arm way too tight.
Finds the vein, glides the needle in. *I was arrested there.
I was new to the area, I got lost, I was trying to find
the freeway. They wanted my I.D. and proof of insurance.
I was trying to find a job. It cost me eight-hundred bucks.*
My blood fills the vial—a red, black, blue color.

US CITIZEN

In the Lovely Nails Salon in Scappoose Oregon
a golden Hello Kitty raises his red arm over and over
again. Incessantly. In the Viet Beauty magazine
a woman with peaches and cream skin

wears a plaid cap and demonstrates in Vietnamese
how to grow nails covered with yellow, pink and blue
violets. She has violet-colored eyes. Lam
was born in Cambodia, grew up in Vietnam.

Without warning, with a goo covered hand
she pulls out her cell phone and shows me a picture
of a document from the US Immigration Service.
As of today she is a US Citizen.

ANNABEL

Lone Pine, Idaho *IS* the General Store and Café—a sprinkling of small cabins and one trailer. The soda machine is busted. We covet the only shade for miles, relax in plastic lawn chairs, and sip warm crème sodas. Inside the store, a polished wooden bar is covered with plastic bags of groceries—preparations for a guided hunting trip. Behind a collection of pine cones, and a metal gold panning plate, a cougar stares at us from a pen and ink drawing. A sign proclaims *NO Ice*. Annabel, who is seven tells us, *Well maybe there is ice, but maybe not*. She will ask her grandpa. Annabel points to a red-rock ridge. I can't discern caves from shadows of caves. If *I howl at night*, she tells us, *the wolves howl back*.

THE GIRL WITH BIG EYES

whose Native name is *wise little raccoon*
writes poems every day about her father
who is gone, maybe in jail, and draws pictures
of hearts broken in two. Her boyfriend breaks up
with her and she cries and cries and can't stop
and doesn't come to school the next day.
A few weeks later she likes another boy
and cuts class to come into my room and flirt
with him, but today he is absent. She looks so sad.
Her heart is full, as full as the harvest moon
and it breaks, keeps breaking, won't stop breaking.

JIM ON FATHER'S DAY

Jim is trying to give away a bacon and maple scone.
He was given this scone by the proprietor of the café
who then kicked us out because the café was closing.
We sit in the shade at wrought-iron tables
and sip too hot to drink coffee from paper cups.
It is sweltering, but pleasant in the shade. We stare
at the street and baskets of hanging geraniums,
and petunias. Water drips onto the sidewalk
from the scarlet, purple and fuchsia-colored blooms.
No cars pass and fewer people. We sit skinny
white knee to large freckled knee. I reach out
my hand and ask him his name. *Jim.*

Oh, that's my father's name,
It's been two years since he passed.

Jim transferred from college in the 60s to Pacific
University, majored in P.E., and then was a track coach
and taught low level math. *Bonehead Math* he calls it.
I tell him I just retired from teaching. He points
with his chin to sign next door: **My Place, est. 1930.**
When you heard a cue ball sailing past your head
you got out of there. Little guys always wanted to fight
big guys. I was a football player, not a fighter.

I ask him if he has kids. He says his Parkinson's makes
him forget what they are doing. *Two with the first wife*
and two with the second. Then he gets very far away.
Joey, my second died two years ago. His liver blew up.
I figure you can't tell them what to do, live their lives
for them. They're going to do what they do. My father
was an alcoholic. I don't drink at all.

We both stare at the pots of petunias and geraniums
dripping water onto the sidewalk. Two college students
walk by. *I bet those kids would like a maple bacon*
scone, I say. And they do. *I have to get going.*
I shake Jim's hand and wish him a happy Father's Day.

TAHOMA

His first love was this mountain with her robes of white
Only seventeen when he became a climbing guide.
Later, he brought us here to camp in a cabin tent,
Caught trout we cooked up in flour and butter.

Only seventeen when he became a climbing guide.
Gave up mountaineering to marry my mother.
Caught trout we cooked up in flour and butter,
She stayed back, changed her Tampax.

Gave up mountaineering to marry my mother.
We tied bandanas around our heads and walked.
She stayed back to change her Tampax,
We walked the trails built with granite steps.

We tied bandanas around our heads and walked.
He taught us to drink from glacial streams.
We walked the trails built with granite steps,
Just kneel down and swallow the earth's blood.

He taught us to drink from glacial streams.
She wrapped her Tampax in newspaper,
Just kneel down and swallow the earth's blood,
Just kneel down and drink the earth's milk.

She wrapped her Tampax in newspaper.
Water so clear you can see pebbles gleaming,
Just kneel down and drink the earth's milk.
Nothing since has ever tasted so sweet.

BLACK ICE

Fifty years ago today, JFK was shot
Flags at half-mast whip in brisk air.
Driving to work: sun glare,
Possibility of a strike, black ice.

The flags at half-mast whip in brisk air.
Fifty years ago I was eight.
Possibility of a strike, black ice.
My parents' marriage slipping off a cliff.

Fifty years ago today I was eight.
My father driving to the mountains
My parents' marriage slipping off a cliff
Telling us be careful, you never know.

My father driving to the mountains
You might hit a patch of black ice
Telling us be careful, you never know
My mom crying, the whole world crying.

You might hit a patch of black ice
Winter break and we were going skiing
My mom crying, the whole world crying.
The highball splashes, a class filled with ice.

Winter break and we were going skiing
Sent home from school early
The highball splashes in a glass filled with ice.
Going slow around the curves in the shade.

Fifty years ago today JFK was shot
Driving to work: sun glare, possibility of black ice.

Minnie B. Stastny c. 1918

Elaine Nussbaum was born in Seattle, and graduated from Mercer Island High School in 1973. Her mother enrolled her in her first creative writing class when she was just seven, and her first poems were published in *Nightshade*, the Mercer Island High Literary magazine. She graduated from Bellevue Community College and the University of Washington with a Bachelor of Arts in Social Work. While attending the University of Washington she studied poetry with Nelson Bentley and David Wagoner.

At her first job, working with runaway youth in Seattle, Ms. Nussbaum began teaching informal poetry therapy groups. She moved to Boulder, Colorado in 1979, and attended the Naropa Institute (now Naropa University), earning a Certificate in Writing from the Jack Kerouac School of Disembodied Poetics at Naropa. She studyed with Anne Waldman, Reed Bye, Anselm Hollo, Jack Collom and Allen Ginsberg.

In 1986, Ms. Nussbaum was a participant on the Great Peace March for Global Nuclear Disarmament—a 2,000-mile march from LA to DC. After the organizer of the Great Peace March, David Mixner went bankrupt two weeks after the March began, leaving 1,200 marchers stranded in the desert near Barstow California, they reorganized and continued 600 strong. No one in Boulder knew whether the Marchers would continue (this was well before cellphones or high speed internet), but miraculously they appeared in Colorado that May. Ms. Nussbaum accompanied Allen Ginsberg on a day-trip to meet the Marchers near Georgetown Lake, Colorado, where he recited his poem "Howl." Ms. Nussbaum joined the March herself later that summer and walked from just west of Chicago to Washington DC.

Ms. Nussbaum attended Portland State University in 1992, studying Special Education, and worked as a Special Education teacher from 1993 until 2016. The highlight of her teaching career was teaching poetry and photography. before you had to be certified in those areas to teach them. She returned to school in 2010, to a low-residency Master of Fine Arts in Writing program at Pacific University, earning her MFA in 2013. She continues to work as a substitute teacher, and occasionally teaches poetry and lyrics at a juvenile detention center in Portland, Oregon. Currently she lives in Scappoose, Oregon with her husband, her cat Squeak, her hen Rocky and her rooster Echinacea.

Ms. Nussbaum's work has appeared in *Poetry Seattle, Bombay Gin, Dog River Review, The Sun, Spilt Infinitive, Louisiana Literature, Women on the Brink, Silk Road,* and *Thimbleberry.* Her chapbook, *Poems in the Key of D-Flat* was published in 1992

Ms. Nussbaum's biggest influences were her mother, Bertha Rose Stastny Houser, who earned a law degree at the University of Washington in the 1960's and was involved in the civil rights movement in Alabama and Washington State, and her father, James Alfred Nussbaum who, while still in high school was a climbing guide on Mt. Rainier, then joined the 10th Mountain Division and served in Italy during WWII.

Printed in the USA
CPSIA information can be obtained
at www.ICGtesting.com
LVHW022055280524
781600LV00005B/249